CUTTING UP WITH PAPER

A Craft Book

Cutting Up With Paper

A CRAFT BOOK

By Peter and Carol Weiss

illustrated by Sally Gralla

Lothrop, Lee & Shepard Co. / New York

Other books by Peter Weiss

BALSA WOOD CRAFT

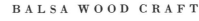

Library of Congress Catalog Card Number 73-4955

1 2 3 4 5 77 76 75 74 73

ISBN 0-688-41561-X   0-688-51561-4 (lib bdg.)

CONTENTS

CUTTING UP WITH PAPER
A Craft Book

TOOLS AND MATERIALS

Paper—One of the best things about using paper as a craft material is that it doesn't cost very much. You can experiment freely without fear of wasting materials if one of your designs doesn't work out right on the first try. For complicated projects you can even cut out practice patterns of newspaper to make sure all the parts will fit together correctly.

Paper comes in a wide variety of colors, sizes, and textures. Art supply stores sell glossy, dull, and bumpy surfaced paper, paper so thin it's almost transparent, corrugated paper, rice paper, rag paper, all kinds of paper. Where should you begin?

Start with a package of ordinary construction paper. Make a few of the simple objects in the chapter on basic techniques. Look through the book and try some projects that call for the use of construction paper. Buy other kinds of paper when you need them for a project. Feel free to substitute one paper for another, but use common sense. Thin tissue paper cannot take the place of heavy poster board in a construction requiring strength.

Some projects specify only the general type of paper needed— light, medium, or heavy weight. The choice you make depends on the color, pattern, and surface texture you want the finished product to have. The wide range of choices adds to the fun of working with paper. Tissue paper, typing paper, and gift wrap paper are some of the lightweight kinds available. Construction paper is medium weight, and comes in several sizes and assorted colors. Heavy papers include oaktag, bristol board, poster board, and watercolor paper. Cardboard, too, is just another thick, strong variety of paper.

There are also special papers that come in handy for certain craft projects. Crepe paper and silver or gold wrapping paper are good for party decorations. Tracing paper and carbon paper are used for transferring patterns to be cut out. Kraft paper (brown) and butcher paper (white) come in long rolls, 3 or 4 feet wide, and are useful for making costumes. Aluminum foil, colored cellophane, waxed paper, and paper straws, plates, and cups are some other materials you might need.

Discount stores and five-and-ten-cent stores sell paper in many of their departments. Look at the school, office, and household supplies, and in the gift or holiday department. For a greater choice of sizes and colors, go to an art-supply store. If there is a college or university near you, look in the bookstore. College bookstores often have excellent art and craft supplies.

Sometimes you won't have to buy paper at all—there is so much you can get free. You might notice that an old paper shopping bag has just the right red and white stripes that you need for a circus tent, or that a shoebox and one or two empty oatmeal boxes can form the basic shapes for a paper castle.

Tools—Many of the tools you will need are probably in your house right now. Scissors and a stapler are the tools most commonly used. Buy these in a store that sells school supplies, if you don't already have them. The list of materials needed at the beginning of each chapter does not include scissors or staplers, since you have to have both before you can start in paper craft at all. A ruler and a compass are two more items you'll need right away to begin making basic paper shapes.

A few projects require the use of a single-edged razor blade or an x-acto knife (available in hardware and hobby shops). Handle sharp blades carefully, and store them in a safe place.

Other Supplies—Paper clips, paper fasteners, pipe cleaners,

10

string, yarn, thread, tape, and glue are all sold in five-and-tens and department stores. Glue and tape are essential. The rest can be bought when they are needed.

A white glue, such as Elmer's, is best for working with paper. This glue comes in a small squeeze bottle with a spout, and is easily washed off your hands and clothing with warm water.

The best tape is called Magic Tape. It is not shiny like other cellophane tape, so it becomes almost invisible when you smooth it down on the paper. For spots where the tape doesn't show, or where more strength is needed, use plain brown masking tape. Get a small roll of each kind of tape. The question of when to use each of the three main fastening methods—glue, tape, and staples—is explored in the next chapter.

Felt-tipped markers, crayons, and paint are good for adding color and detail. But the patterns and color contrasts of different types of paper can provide brightness and variety even with no other decoration.

Papier-maché projects call for special equipment. The main ingredient is just old newspapers, but you also need a cheap plastic bucket, a plastic bowl, water-soluble paints, two or three paint brushes of different sizes, wheat paste, and a small jar of acrylic medium.

Acrylic medium is a white liquid that dries to form a colorless, transparent film. Papier-mâché creations should be covered with a layer of acrylic medium before being painted. Acrylic paints are easy to use, quick-drying, and give a tough, waterproof finish. Poster or tempera paints are easy to use. But the colors are not as bright as acrylics and take longer to dry.

Most papier-mâché supplies, including paint and brushes, can be bought cheaply in a discount store or five-and-ten. To find acrylic medium you may have to go to an art-supply store. Hardware stores sell wheat paste (a white powder, like flour).

BASIC TECHNIQUES

Folding and Scoring—Most kinds of paper are easy to fold. Use a ruler to draw a very light pencil line, then crease the paper along the line. To fold stiff paper, just hold the edge of the ruler at the line and bend the paper back over the ruler.

Scoring is another way of handling difficult folds. Put some newspaper under the paper you're working on. Go over the line to be folded with a dull tool, like the rounded point of a butter knife or a ball-point pen that has run out of ink. Press hard enough to make a slight groove in the paper. It will now fold easily along the scored line.

Curling—Curling is a way of making flat pieces of paper take on a permanent curved shape. Cut two strips of paper about an inch wide and several inches long. Roll up one strip and set it down on the table. The natural springiness of the paper will make it unroll again. Take the other strip and pull it tightly down over the edge of the table. This process stretches one side of the paper and gives it a permanent curl. Try curling other strips. You'll find that the tightness of the curl depends on the weight of the paper and how hard you pull it against the edge of the table.

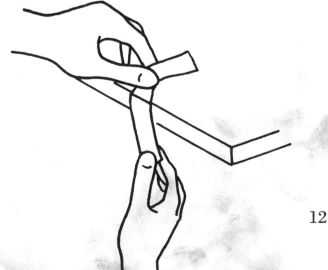

Transferring Patterns—Sometimes you will want to trace a pattern from the book and transfer it to a sheet of paper. Put a piece of tracing paper on top of the pattern and go over the lines with a soft pencil. Put a piece of carbon paper, shiny-side down, on top of the paper you're going to use for your project. Put the tracing paper on top of the carbon paper. Go over the tracing again with the pencil, pressing hard enough so that the pattern comes through on the bottom sheet of paper.

Fastening—Which should you use—staples, tape, or glue? Each has advantages and disadvantages. Sometimes only one method of fastening will work in a particular project, but usually you have a choice. Try all three and you will be able to decide which you prefer.

Staples provide the easiest and quickest way of holding paper together securely. If you're working with complicated paper shapes, though, you may not be able to fit the stapler into the right position on the paper. Staples can cause rips in lightweight, delicate paper, and you may not want staples showing on the finished project. When these problems come up, you'll have to use tape or glue.

Often it is possible to put a piece of tape in a spot where your stapler cannot reach. Tape is convenient because it is flexible. It bends around corners and follows the shape of the paper. The biggest disadvantage of tape is that it can dry out with age and lose its holding power.

With glue you don't have to worry about that. Two pieces of paper properly glued together will never fall apart. Spread a very thin layer of glue on both of the surfaces to be joined. Press them together gently but firmly, and wait for the glue to dry. It is important not to use too much glue or the paper will warp and start to look sloppy. It may help to squeeze out a drop on a small paintbrush and spread the glue with the brush. Glue can be messy and it takes a little longer, but it is the strongest and most permanent fastening technique.

Cylinders—Take a sheet of paper and roll it up loosely, the long way. Fasten the ends together to make a cylinder. Another piece of paper, the same size as the first but rolled up the short way, will make a cylinder of a completely different size. You can get other sizes by rolling the paper tightly in a tube, or by rolling up a long strip into a hoop or ring. Cylinders of all types are used in paper-craft projects. Remember that it's easier to roll paper up smoothly if you curl it slightly first. Plan your work so that staples or tape will be in back where they won't show.

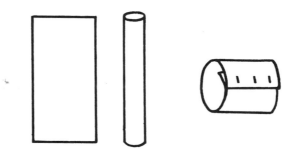

Cones—Use a compass to draw a circle on a sheet of paper. Cut out the circle. Make a cut from one edge to the center. Overlap the cut edges and staple them together. The circle is changed into a three-dimensional shape—a wide, flat cone.

Draw and cut out another circle. This time, cut away one third of the circle, as if you were taking a large slice out of a pie. The shape of the cones you make depends on what part of the circle you start with. A cone made from two thirds of a circle will be a little higher and more pointed than the one made from a full circle. Use just one third of the circle and you will get a tall, sharp cone.

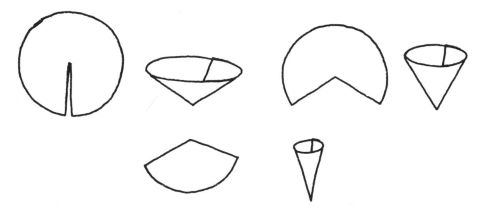

Boxes—Using a ruler, draw a pattern of 3 inch squares, like the small pattern in the top illustration. Cut out the pattern, crease it on the lines, and fold it into a box. Fasten the edges together with tape. This pattern can be varied to make any shape box from a single sheet of paper. Look at the jack-in-the-box on page 19.

To get neater-looking results, put the tape on the inside. For a stronger box, use small tabs of paper instead of tape. Just fold them so that they fit inside the corners of the box. Hold them in place with glue.

The best-looking and sturdiest boxes are made by planning a pattern that includes folding tabs, like the one in the bottom illustration. It takes longer to draw the pattern this way, but putting the box together will be a lot easier.

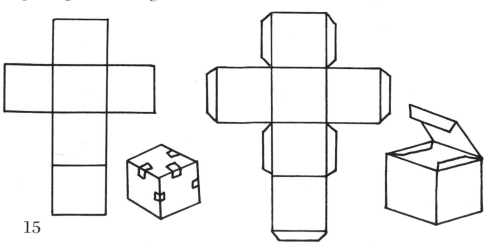

TOYS

Pinwheel

Materials Needed:
a square piece of paper
a new, unsharpened pencil, with eraser
a thumbtack

How to Make It:
1. Draw straight lines connecting opposite corners of the square piece of paper.
2. Starting from each corner, cut the paper almost all the way in to the center. Fold half of each corner in to the center. Hold the points in place with tape.
3. Push the thumbtack through the center of the pinwheel and into the eraser on the pencil. Blow on the pinwheel to make it spin.

Other Possibilities:
Glue paper streamers to the points of the pinwheel, and decorate it with cut-out paper polka dots.

Make the windmill on the next page.

Windmill

Materials Needed:
a large paper or styrofoam cup
construction paper
a thumbtack
felt-tipped markers

How to Make It:
1. Turn the cup upside down. Draw a door and windows with colored markers.
2. Make the roof from a low, flat cone (see p. 14), glued on top of the upside-down cup. If you want shingles on the roof, you can glue on overlapping squares of colored paper, or overlapping rows of paper strips with slits along their bottom edges. Start gluing the shingles at the bottom edge of the roof and work your way up to the top.
3. Make a pinwheel from a 3 inch square of paper. Use the thumbtack to attach the pinwheel to the cup. If you want a base, glue the windmill to a sheet of paper.

Other Possibilities:
Combine paper cups with oatmeal boxes and other empty kitchen cartons to get the basic shape of any type of building you want to make. Try making a lighthouse, a firehouse, a castle, or a cathedral.

17

Helicopter

Materials Needed:
colored paper
paper clips

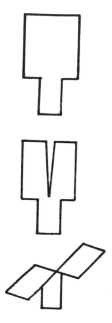

How to Make It:
1. Cut a piece of paper the same shape as the top illustration. Make it any size you want, as long as the shape is the same.
2. Cut a slit down the center of the top part.
3. Fold down the wings in opposite directions. Glue a few colored paper dots onto the wings.
4. Attach a paper clip to the bottom. If the helicopter is a big one, you might need to use two or three paper clips. Throw the helicopter high in the air and it will spin gently to the ground.

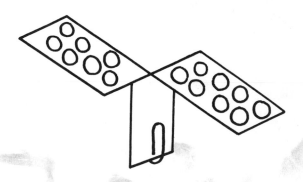

Jack-in-the-Box

Materials Needed:
oaktag or some other thick paper
crayons, paints, or felt-tipped markers

How to Make It:
1. Make a small, shallow box like the
one shown.
2. Cut a strip of paper ½ inch wide and
about 4 inches long. Fold it back and
forth into eight or nine accordion folds.
Glue one end inside the box. Cut out a
paper head and draw or paint a funny
face on it. Glue the head to the other end
of the folded strip.
3. Fold the strip and the head flat inside
the box. When you open the lid, the jack-
in-the-box pops out.

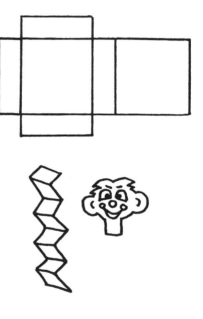

Other Possibilities:
Make greeting cards with figures mounted
on folded paper springs that pop up when
the cards are opened.

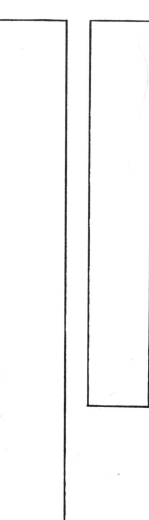

Ring Wing Plane

Materials Needed:

a paper or plastic drinking straw
a sheet of lightweight paper (typing or
   notebook paper)
tracing paper and carbon paper

How to Make It:

1. Trace the two strip patterns and transfer them to the paper. Cut out the strips.
2. Roll one strip into a ring and glue the ends together. Do the same thing with the other strip. Glue one ring to each end of the straw.

To fly the plane, hold the straw with the small ring in front. Throw the plane lightly and watch it sail through the air.

Streamlined Straw Plane

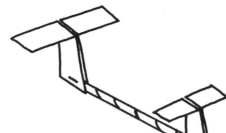

Materials Needed.

a paper drinking straw or a tightly rolled
tube of lightweight paper if you can't
find paper straws
a sheet of construction paper
tracing paper and carbon paper

How to Make It:

1. Fold the construction paper in half.
Trace and transfer the wing patterns on
page 20 to the paper, with the dark lines
along the fold. Cut out the wings.

2. Flatten the straw. Put one end of the
straw inside the fold of the front wings
and staple it in place. Do the same thing
to attach the rear wings.

3. Staple the wings together just below
the dotted lines. Fold the wings down
along the dotted lines.

Other Possibilities:

Try out your own wing designs in different shapes and sizes until you get a
plane that will fly. If a plane dives too
sharply, try making the front wings bigger. If it points its nose up and stalls,
make the rear wings a little bigger or attach a paper clip to the front of the wings.

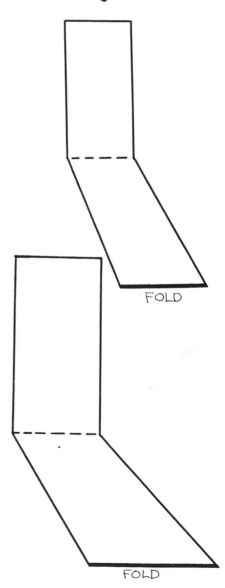

FOLD

FOLD

Covered Wagon

Materials Needed:

a shoebox
several sheets of typing paper or a 12 by 24 inch sheet of white
   paper
thick cardboard
round-headed paper fasteners
paint, markers, or crayons

How to Make It:

1. Cut four cardboard circles, each 5 inches across. Make holes in the centers. Paint or draw rims and spokes.
2. Punch two holes in each side of the shoebox, near the lower corners. Attach wheels with paper fasteners.
3. Glue together the ends of enough sheets of typing paper to make a piece 24 inches long and as wide as the length of the shoebox. If you have a large sheet, cut it to the right size, double it and glue one end inside each side of the shoebox.
4. Cut a strip of cardboard 1 by 10 or 12 inches. Cut another strip 1 by 7 inches. Glue the strips together in the shape of a cross. With a paper fastener or glue attach the cross under the front of the wagon.

Other Possibilities:

Try a locomotive, several boxcars, and a caboose, all made from shoeboxes and attached together to form a train, or a truck, bus, doll carriage, or any other vehicle you want to make.

Frontier Fort

Materials Needed:
a sheet of oaktag
two or three boxes of drinking straws
scraps of paper
an x-acto knife or single-edged razor blade
two pipe cleaners
paints and brushes

How to Make It:
1. The side and back walls of the fort are made of straws that have been cut in half. You could cut them one at a time, with scissors, but the fastest way is to put a whole box of straws on a cutting board or kitchen counter and slice it in half with a sharp knife.
2. Line up a row of half straws about 10 or 12 inches long. Cut a 2 inch wide strip of oaktag the same length as the row of straws. Put a thin coat of glue on the strip, turn it over, and press it down on the straws. Let the glue dry for several hours.
3. Repeat the same process to make two more low walls. Make the fourth wall for the front of the fort, with a 4 inch section of uncut straws in the center. Use a short strip of oaktag to give extra strength to the high part of the wall.

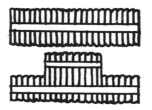

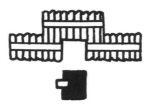

4. Cut a doorway in the front wall with an x-acto knife or razor blade. Cut an oaktag door to fit in the opening and attach it with a hinge of tape. Make the flagpoles out of pipecleaners, with paper flags glued on.

5. Fasten the walls together at the corners with paper tabs. Glue the fort to the middle of the remaining oaktag. Paint the fort brown so that the straws look like logs. Paint the oaktag base green.

Other Possibilities:

Use corrugated cardboard instead of straws to give the appearance of log walls.

Make log houses, barns, and corrals to use with the fort in a complete model of an early frontier settlement.

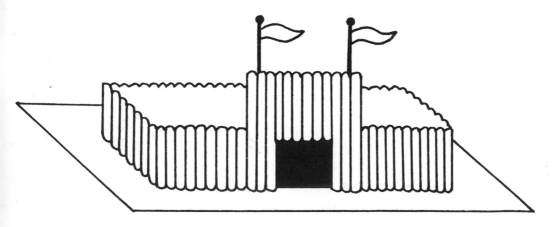

ART
Paper Collage

Materials Needed:
a piece of sturdy cardboard or poster board
colored paper (any kind)

How to Make It:
1. A collage is any design made by pasting or gluing various materials on a flat surface. You can create an abstract design, concentrating on patterns and colors, or you can arrange the paper shapes to make a picture of something.
2. Cut a few simple shapes out of colored paper and put them on top of the cardboard background. Move them around until you like the way they look. Cut more pieces in different colors and place them on the cardboard, too. When you have all the pieces where you want them, just glue them in place.

Other Possibilities:
Tear the paper to get shapes without sharp, cut edges.

Make a collage with layers of colored tissue paper, so that the bottom colors can be seen through the layers on top of them.

Use bits of string, wool, cellophane, crepe paper, or other materials to make the collage look more interesting.

Make a collage using only white paper, but in a wide variety of textures. Use thick white cardboard, tracing paper, waxed paper, different types of drawing paper, and paper napkins, towels, and tissues. You can add texture to plain paper by cutting rows of slits, punching holes, or crumpling the paper and then flattening it out again.

25

Opposite-Color Cutouts

Materials Needed:
colored paper (light or medium weight)

How to Make It:
1. Pick two sheets of paper in colors that go well together. Put aside one sheet to use as a background. Cut the other sheet in half.

2. Fold one of the half sheets in half, then fold it in half again. Cut out interesting shapes from the corners or edges of the folded paper. Open up and flatten out the folded paper and the scraps cut from it.

3. Make a two-sided design by gluing the scraps to one half of the background, and

gluing the piece they were cut from to the other half. The design in the illustration has black paper on top of a white background. The cut-off scraps of black paper have been glued to the right side of the background.

Other Possibilities:

For a really intricate design, use very thin paper, folded in half three or four times. Cut lots of small pieces from the edges and corners with manicure scissors.

Use a background of colored tissue and tape the finished design to a windowpane for a stained-glass look.

Ink Blowing

Materials Needed:
paper with a smooth, glossy finish
a drinking straw
ink

How to Make It:
1. Use a toothpick or match to put one or two drops of ink on a sheet of paper.
2. Blow lightly through the straw to make the ink move around on the paper. At first you may have some trouble making the ink go where you want, but a little practice helps a lot. Start with abstract designs. When you can control the movement of the ink you'll be able to do many different kinds of pictures.

Other Possibilities:
Glue flat paper cutouts to an oaktag base. When the glue is dry, blow ink around the edges of the cutouts.

Find a ball-point pen that has run out of ink. Put an old magazine under the paper and press hard with the pen to engrave a design on the paper. Blow ink along the engraved lines.

28

Paper Weaving

Materials Needed:
sheets of colored paper
an x-acto knife or single-edged razor blade

How to Make It:
1. Draw a very light pencil line across each end of a sheet of paper, 1 inch from the edge.
2. Spread out a thick pad of newspaper or a magazine to use as a cutting surface. Make a row of cuts connecting the two pencil lines. Straight, evenly spaced cuts will result in a weaving with a checkerboard pattern. Unevenly spaced cuts that curve or zigzag will give the weaving more variety.
3. Cut strips of paper in different colors and widths, but all the same length as the two pencil lines you drew.
4. Weave the strips in and out through the cuts in the first sheet of paper. You may have to trim the last strip to make it fit.

Other Possibilities:
Weave in a few strips of ribbon, fabric, or yarn, along with paper strips.

Experiment with different kinds of paper and various color schemes. Try using strips of crepe paper or wrapping paper with a bright pattern. Sometimes a good design results from using lots of different colors, sometimes from using just two or three colors.

Butterfly Mobile

Materials Needed:

tissue paper

scraps of aluminum foil and bright wrapping paper

thread

pipe cleaners

a thin dowel rod (available in hardware stores)

How to Make It:

1. Cut six or seven small butterfly shapes of colored tissue paper. Decorate the wings by gluing on pieces of wrapping paper and aluminum foil. Make each butterfly different.

2. Make bodies by bending pipe cleaners in half and spreading the ends to look like antennas. Tie a piece of thread to each body. Glue the bodies to the centers of the butterflies.

3. Tie the threads to the dowel rod. Make sure that the threads are different lengths, so the butterflies won't all be hanging at the same level.

4. Tie a long piece of thread to the middle of the dowel rod. Lift the mobile by this thread to see if it is balanced. Move the knot back and forth until the dowel hangs without tipping. Put a little glue on the knot so the thread won't slip. Hang the mobile from the ceiling.

Other Possibilities:

Make birds or fish instead of butterflies.

Make a mobile using abstract shapes or origami figures (see p. 36).

Make a holiday mobile using paper stars (see p. 48).

Paper Bouquet

Materials Needed:
construction paper
colored tissue paper or crepe paper
drinking straws or pipe cleaners

How to Make It:
1. Cut a few flower shapes out of construction paper, in different colors and sizes. Curl the petals slightly so they'll look more lifelike. Glue the end of a straw or pipe cleaner to the back of each flower.
2. There are several ways to make centers for the flowers. The easiest technique is to cut colored-paper circles and make cuts around the outside of each circle. Bend the edges up in a fringe and glue a circle in the center of each flower. Another way is to cut a long strip of tissue or crepe paper, make little cuts along one side of the strip, and then roll it up as tightly as possible and glue it to a flower.
3. Cut green paper leaves with a long thin tab sticking out at the base of each leaf. Curl the leaves very lightly over the edge of a table. Put glue on the tabs and wrap them around the straw or pipe cleaner stems. If you want some flowers to be taller than the rest, just twist two

32

pipe cleaners together or join two straws with tape.

4. The vase is a small cylinder of construction paper. Cut a paper bottom for the vase and attach it with tape or tabs. Paint the vase, or decorate it with colored-paper cutouts. Put a few pebbles in the vase so that it won't tip over. Arrange the flowers in the vase.

Other Possibilities:

Make small paper-flower place tags for a party.

A Christmas wreath with paper branches, leaves, and berries on a doughnut-shaped cardboard framework is a great holiday decoration.

Japanese Lanterns

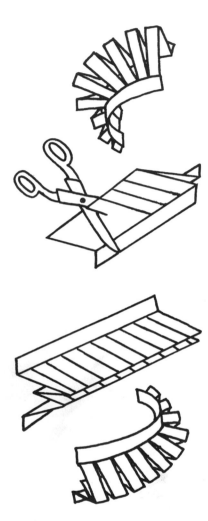

Materials Needed:
sheets of lightweight colored paper
paper clips
strong thread

How to Make It:
1. Lay a rectangle of paper out flat on the table. Fold up a strip about 1 inch wide along each long side of the paper. Fold the whole sheet in half, lengthwise, with the two folded-up strips on the outside.
2. Make a row of parallel cuts from the center fold right up to the folded strips. Closely spaced cuts make a delicate lantern, and widely spaced cuts make a strong, sturdy one.
3. Open up the paper partway and roll it into a cylinder. The top diagram shows the paper partly rolled, with the row of cut strips just beginning to fan out. Bring the ends around until they overlap slightly and fasten them together.
4. Tie a paper clip to each end of a piece of strong thread. Attach the paper clips to one end of the lantern and hang it from the ceiling or in a doorway.

Other Possibilities:
The bottom diagram shows how to vary

the shape of the lantern by changing the way you fold the paper.

Roll a cylinder of colored tissue paper or cellophane just big enough to fit inside the lantern. Attach it at the top with paper clips. This type of lantern looks really nice if it's used as a lampshade, with the light shining through the colored paper.

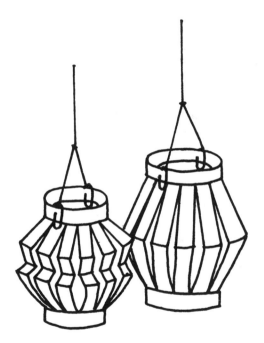

Origami Swan

Origami is the Japanese name for a special kind of papercraft. Origami projects are usually made from a single square of paper. Origami looks more complicated than it really is. Once you have tried it you will see that it isn't very hard at all. The swan is made in eight steps. The illustrations on these two pages show how the paper should look after each step.

Material Needed:
an 8 inch square of lightweight paper

How to Make It:
1. Crease the square down the middle from one corner to the opposite corner. Open it up again and spread it out flat.
2. Fold one corner in to the center crease.
3. Fold in the opposite corner the same way. This will leave you with a shape that looks like an upside-down kite.
4. Fold one corner of the kite shape in to the center crease.
5. Fold in the opposite corner the same way. This will produce a diamond shape.

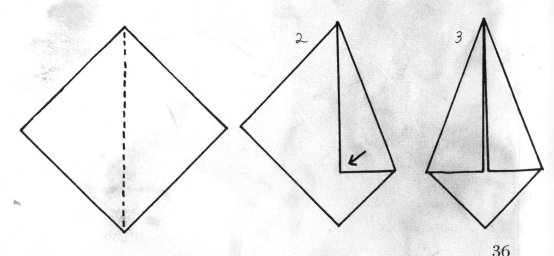

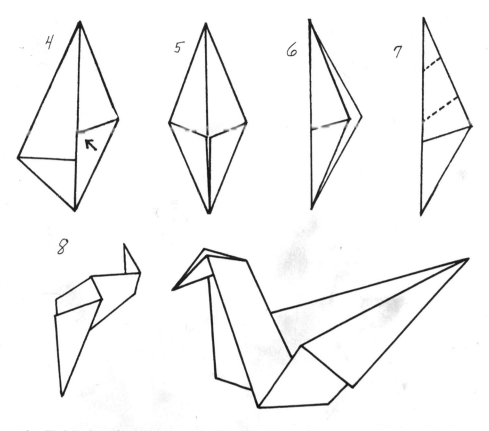

6. Fold the diamond in half, bending the center crease backward.

7. Draw light pencil lines, as shown by the dotted lines in the diagram. Crease both ways on the pencil lines to soften the paper.

8. Make the head and neck by folding along the penciled lines, reversing the direction of the center crease in the area between the two lines.

Other Possibilities:

If you enjoyed making the swan and want to try other projects, look in the library for books on origami. You can learn to make boxes, baskets, fish, birds, and animals, all by folding a single sheet of paper.

HOLIDAY CREATIONS
Greeting Cards

Materials Needed:
colored paper

How to Make It:
1. Cut rectangles of paper a little less than twice the size of the envelopes you plan to use. Fold each rectangle in half. What you do next depends on what kinds of cards you want to make. Three types you can make are shown here, but the real fun is to dream up your own designs.

2. In the illustrated Christmas card a tree shape is cut out of the front of the card. The message inside can be read when the card is closed. For other holidays, cut out the shape of a pumpkin, turkey, Valentine heart, and so on.

3. The birthday card has a separate piece inside, in the shape of a boy's head and arms. Glue the center of this separate piece to the center of the card, right on the fold. Do not put glue on the arms or hands. When the card is opened, the boy waves his arms happily.

4. The third card has a paper flower mounted on a folded paper spring (see p. 19). The flower pops up when you open the card.

Other Possibilities:

Make a stencil by cutting a design out of a piece of heavy paper. Put the stencil on top of the cards, one at a time, paint over it and the design will be repeated.

Create holiday pictures by cutting and gluing scraps of colored paper on the front and inside of each card.

Christmas Snow Flakes

Materials Needed:
construction paper
colored cellophane or tissue paper
Magic Tape

How to Make It:

FOLD

FOLD

1. Cut a square or a circle of construction paper. Fold it in half, then in half again. Cut out small pieces, in various shapes, from the edges and corners of the folded paper.

2. Unfold the snowflake and flatten it out. Cut a piece of cellophane or tissue paper the right size and shape to cover the snowflake completely. Tape the cellophane to the snowflake and hang it on a windowpane with a small piece of tape.

Valentine Cutouts

Materials Needed:
pink or white construction paper
red cellophane
Magic Tape
an x-acto knife or single-edged razor blade

How to Make It:
1. Since Valentine shapes are not as symmetrical as snowflakes, it's easier to cut them out without folding the paper. Make a few sketches on scrap paper until you decide on a design. Draw the design lightly in pencil on the construction paper.

2. Protect the table with a cutting board or an old magazine. Cut around the outlines of your design with an x-acto knife or single-edged razor. Cover the cutout with cellophane, and hang it in window.

Other Possibilities:
Cutouts made with a knife or a razor can be big and bold or lacy and delicate, with hundreds of tiny holes forming patterns on the paper. Try using black paper and cellophane in several different colors to get a stained-glass window effect.

Small snowflakes cut from colored paper can be dabbed with glue, sprinkled with gold or silver glitter, and used as Christmas tree decorations.

41

Easter Candy Cup

Materials Needed:

heavy white drawing paper or thin oaktag
  paper
construction paper
several sheets of tissue paper

How to Make It:

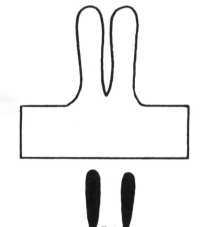

1. Draw the pattern for the rabbit's body on the white paper. All you have to do is draw a strip across one end of the paper, with the long ears sticking up in the middle.

2. Cut out the pattern and roll it up into a cylinder. Curl the paper first if it seems too stiff to roll up easily. Fasten the cylinder with glue or staples.

3. Cut a triangle of red or pink construction paper for the nose, and two long, red teardrop shapes to represent the insides of the ears. Cut construction paper eyes and whiskers, in whatever colors you want. Glue all these paper shapes in place on the rabbit.

4. Cut a round bottom to fit the candy cup, using a scrap of white paper or bristol board. Attach it securely, on the inside of the cup, with bent paper tabs or pieces of tape.

5. Cut the colored tissue paper into very

thin strips. Fill the cup halfway with crumpled tissue strips. Fill it the rest of the way with jelly beans, chocolate eggs, and other Easter candies.

Other Possibilities:
Make a whole family of Easter bunnies in different sizes, shapes, and colors.

A hollow ghost, witch, or cat, will hold your Halloween treats.

If you make small, hollow animal party favors, you can put a piece of candy or an inexpensive gift inside each one.

Halloween Monster Masks

Materials Needed:
large paper grocery bags
construction paper
a crayon or a piece of chalk

How to Make It:
1. Put a paper bag over your head. Use a crayon or chalk to mark where to cut holes for your eyes. Do not use a pencil or any other sharp object.

2. Take off the bag and cut out small eyeholes.

3. Use construction paper to make horns, ears, fangs, and whatever other features you want. Long, narrow paper cones make good horns or noses. Other features can be made from flat or curled shapes.

4. Enlarge the eyeholes so that you can see easily through them. Make construction paper eyes, with holes in the middle and glue them over the eyeholes.

Other Possibilities:
Make a bird mask, with a long, sharp beak and overlapping layers of paper feathers.

Make an animal mask, using overlapping layers of curled paper strips to look like fur. Leave the face part without fur, and make a muzzle by gluing on a low, wide cone.

Turkey Centerpiece

Materials Needed:
construction paper

How to Make It:
1. Roll a sheet of construction paper into a cylinder. Fasten it with tape or staples. Flatten the cylinder slightly and cut out the turkey's body, outlined by a dotted line in the small illustration. Round out the cylinder again.

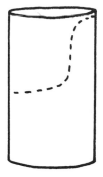

2. The tail is a paper circle glued or stapled to the back of the body. Cut paper feathers and glue them to the tail in a fan pattern. Use fall colors.
3. Cut two wings of colored paper and glue them to the sides of the body. Glue small paper feathers onto the wings.
4. Cut out a beak, eyes, and a wattle (the red fold of skin that hangs down the front of the turkey's neck). Glue these pieces in place.

Other Possibilities:
Make the body of stronger paper, put a bottom on it, and fill with nuts or candy.

Make a Pilgrim figure to go with the turkey. Look in the Paper People chapter to get ideas on how to make it. Look in an encyclopedia for details of Pilgrim clothing.

Folded Angels

Materials Needed:

medium-weight paper (silver paper is attractive, but any kind will do)

Christmas wrapping paper

How to Make It:

1. Fold a sheet of paper in half. Draw one of the angel patterns, or make up one of your own. Cut the angel out. Don't forget to cut out the mouth.

2. Unfold the angel partway, so that it will stand up. Curl the arms forward and the wings backward.

3. Cut ten or twenty small, thin strips of wrapping paper. Roll one strip into a ring and glue the ends together. Put another strip through the first one, then roll it into a ring. Keep adding links until your chain is the right length to fit around the angel's neck.

Other Possibilities:

Make an angel by starting with a cone. (Look at the gypsy doll on p. 52.) This kind of angel will look good at the top of the Christmas tree.

Make paper chains to drape around the tree. The work goes faster if you use bigger strips.

Silver Stars

Materials Needed:
silver wrapping paper
Magic Tape
thread

How to Make It:
1. Cut a 10 by 12 inch rectangle of silver paper for each star you want to make. Fold each rectangle into accordion folds 1 inch wide, starting from one short end.
2. Staple the folded paper together at the center. Cut a triangular section from each end of the folded paper, as shown by the dotted lines in the illustration.
3. Fan out one end of the paper to make half of the star. Fan out the other end to make the other half. Staple or tape the halves of the star together.
4. Glue a circle of silver paper to the center of the star. Turn the star over and glue a circle to the other side, too. Use a big loop of thread, attached with tape, to hang the star on the tree.

Other Possibilities:
Decorate the star by cutting rows of small notches in the edges of the folded paper. This produces a star with an open, airy look.

Make more stars in different sizes, using brightly patterned holiday wrapping paper.

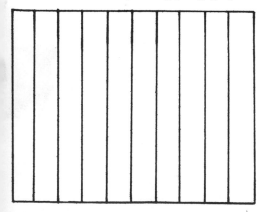

Three Wise Men

Materials Needed:
paper or styrofoam cups
construction paper
gift wrapping paper (three different patterns)
string

How to Make It:
1. Make a small hole in the bottom of each cup. Cut three long pieces of string and push one through the hole in each cup. Tie knots in the string so that you can hang the cups upside down.
2. To make the robes, roll up three rectangles of wrapping paper and glue them to the rims of the cups. Scratch the cups with a compass point so that the glue will hold better.
3. Glue on strips of construction paper for hair, beards, and mustaches after scratching the surfaces of the cups. Cut out eyes and noses and glue them on. Cut and glue on construction paper crowns, in different shapes.
4. Hang the Three Wise Men on your Christmas tree.

Other Possibilities:
Make hair and beads of colored yarn or string. Use silver or gold paper for the crowns.

Make a paper cup Santa with red cheeks and a white beard, dressed in a red coat with white trim.

Make hanging angels with long, silver-paper robes and feathery wings of colored tissue paper.

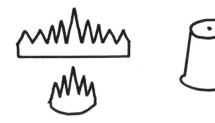

PAPER PEOPLE

Finger Puppets

Materials Needed:
colored paper
pieces of string or yarn (optional)

How to Make It:
1. Make two paper cylinders big enough to slip over your fingers.
2. Cut small eyes, noses, and mouths out of colored paper and glue them onto the cylinders. Hair and a mustache can be made from curled strips of paper or from bits of yarn or string.
3. Make collars or clothing by wrapping and gluing a paper strip around the base of each cylinder. Add buttons or bows, or whatever other details you want.
4. Slip the finished puppets onto your fingers and you can put on your own puppet show.

Other Possibilities:
Make puppets with hats, or animal puppets.

Gypsy Doll

Materials Needed:
construction paper
a sheet of gift wrapping paper or some
  other fancy, patterned paper
felt-tipped markers

How to Make It:
1. Use your compass to draw a large circle on a bright-colored sheet of construction paper. Draw another circle, the same size, on a sheet of tan or pink construction paper.

2. Cut the bright colored circle in half and roll the semicircle into a cone (see p. 14). Roll a tall, pointed cone from one third of the tan or pink circle. Fasten both cones securely with staples, tape, or glue. Put the tan or pink cone on top of the colored one and fasten them together with tape.

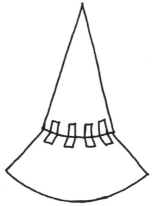

3. Cut a piece of gift wrapping paper to make a shawl that will wrap around the figure and overlap a little in the front. Fasten it together in front with a staple or a little drop of glue. If necessary, trim the shawl to make it shorter than the gypsy's skirt, but leave it long enough to hide the tape.

4. Cut off the tip of the top cone, so the head won't be pointed. Glue on long hair made from thin strips of black or brown paper. Cut two hoop earrings from paper and glue them to the sides of the head. Draw on eyes and other features with felt-tipped markers.

Other Possibilities:

This same kind of construction based on cones can be used to make a policewoman, a princess, or any other figure wearing a dress or long skirt.

Try making a whole family of gypsies. The men and boys could be made the same way as the circus ringmaster (see p. 85), but without the ringmaster's black cape and top hat. Just use brighter colors for the clothing, and tie a small tissue-paper bandanna around the figure's neck.

Pirate Mask

Materials Needed:

a paper plate

a sheet of tissue paper or gift wrapping
   paper

How to Make It:

1. To make the pirate's kerchief, fold the
sheet of tissue paper over the paper plate.
Leave enough tissue at one side of the
plate to be crumpled up to look like a
knot.

2. Fold down one corner of the tissue
behind the plate so the kerchief takes the
rounded shape of the top of the head.
Bunch up the tissue at the other side and
leave it sticking out. Flatten out all the
tissue on the back of the plate and hold
the back part of the kerchief in place with
lots of tape.

3. Cut lots of 2 or 3 inch strips from
construction paper. Curl the strips and
glue them to the edges of the plate to
make the pirate's beard. Glue on a few
strips for each side of the mustache. Use
a strip or two for each eyebrow.

4. There are several ways to make a nose
for the pirate. You can glue on a small
cone or cylinder, cut a folded triangular
shape, or just glue a red circle onto the
paper plate.

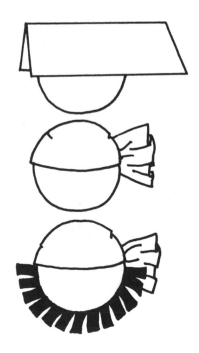

5. Cut out eyes and a big hoop earring from scraps of colored paper and glue them onto the face.

6. If you want to wear the mask, cut out eyeholes and punch holes at the sides for string. Strengthen the string holes with tape or gummed looseleaf reinforcements. If you want to hang the mask on the wall, don't make holes. Just fasten a loop of ribbon or string to the back of the mask, near the top.

Other Possibilities:

Make a crew of pirates with different hair, faces, and hats. They might have eyepatches or hats with a skull and crossbones design.

Make a mask representing each member of your family, including any pets you might have.

Make a princess with a crown and lacy collar, a cowboy, baseball player, nurse, fireman, or anyone with a special type of hat.

King

Materials Needed:

construction paper
a sheet of patterned wrapping paper
a sheet of silver or gold paper

How to Make It:

1. Fold a piece of skin-colored construction paper in half and draw a pattern like the one in the diagram. Cut it out.

2. Unfold the body partway, so it can stand on its feet. Roll both ends of the strip for the head. Fasten it with glue.

3. Cut a rectangle of wrapping paper and put it around the king's shoulders to make a cloak. Staple the ends together.

4. Make the hair by gluing strips of paper to the sides and back of the head. Glue on curled strips to make the beard. Cut out a mustache and two eyes of construction paper. Glue them on.

5. Cut a wide strip of gold or silver paper long enough to fit around the top of the head. Cut out the points of the crown with scissors. Staple it in place, fastening it at the back, where the staple won't show.

Other Possibilities:

A king and queen can be made of rolled paper and masking tape, like the giraffe on p. 68, sitting on two cardboard thrones.

Queen

Materials Needed:
construction paper
a sheet of colorful wrapping paper
a sheet of silver or gold paper
felt-tipped markers

How to Make It:
1. Draw a large half circle on the sheet of wrapping paper. Cut it out and roll it up into a cone. Fasten with tape or staples. Cut off the tip of the cone, leaving a hole about 1 or 2 inches across.
2. Roll skin-colored paper into a cylinder tight enough to fit through the top of the cone. With the cone and the cylinder standing up on end, the cylinder should stick out about 2 inches at the top. Trim either or both parts to get the right proportions.
3. Glue on curled strips of paper to make the hair. Draw the face with felt-tipped markers.
4. To make the crown cut a strip of silver or gold paper with a jagged row of points along the top. Roll it up around the top of the head and glue or staple it together.

Other Possibilities:
Put the queen and the king in a castle made of papier-maché, with a palace guard of knights.

Knight

Materials Needed:
construction paper
a paper straw
a small, thin paint brush

How to Make It:
1. Make the knight's body by rolling up a cylinder of blue or gray paper. Fasten it with staples. Roll two tighter cylinders of paper of the same color. Insert the two tight cylinders into one end of the body. Hold the legs in place with glue.
2. Make the head by rolling a small cylinder of skin-colored paper and inserting it in the top of the body. Fasten it with staples or glue. Glue on eyes and a mustache cut from colored paper.
3. The arms are cut from a single long strip of paper of the same color as the body and legs. Glue the arms to the back of the figure. Curl them slightly so they bend around toward the front of the body.
4. Draw a helmet pattern like the one shown, big enough to fit around the head and overlap a little in back. Cut out the helmet. Fasten the ends together with glue. Bend the four points in toward the center and glue them together. Brush a little glue around the top of the head,

then put the helmet on the head.

5. Cut a paper shield in some bright color. Decorate the shield with glued-on paper shapes. Bend the knight's left arm at the elbow. Glue the shield to the left arm, in front of the body. If the weight of the shield makes the knight fall over, just glue the edge of the shield to the knight's chest.

6. Wrap the knight's right hand around the paper straw. Fasten it with a little glue. Glue a paper flag to the top of the straw.

Other Possibilities:

Make a horse for the knight, like the bareback rider's horse on p. 78.

ANIMALS

Curled Paper Owl

Materials Needed:
construction paper
an x-acto knife or single-edged razor blade
an old magazine or wooden board

How to Make It:
1. Lay a sheet of paper on top of the magazine or board. Use the knife or razor blade to make several rows of V-shaped cuts across the bottom half of the paper.
2. Cut a semicircle from the top of the paper. Curl the paper sideways over the edge of the table (see p. 12). After the paper is curled it will stand up on end.
3. Bend the V-cuts up to look like feathers. Cut eyes and a beak from brightly colored paper and glue them to the owl.

Other Possibilities:
Use this simple technique to make any animal that doesn't have long limbs, or use it to make a sitting animal. Whatever the shape of the animal, if the bottom edge is straight, the paper can be curled to make it stand on its edge. Try a rabbit, a chicken, a cat, or anything else you can think of.

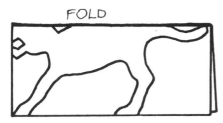

Folded Animals

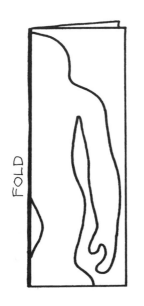

Materials Needed:
medium or heavy weight colored paper
crayons or felt-tipped markers

How to Make It:
1. Fold three sheets of paper in half and draw the three patterns shown in the illustration. Cut out the three animals.
2. Draw dark eyes and stripes on both sides of the tiger. Cut small rounded ears of scrap paper and glue them on the sides of the head.
3. Unfold the gorilla, draw a face on it, and stand it on its feet.
4. Glue the two sides of the deer's head together. Spread the antlers apart.

Other Possibilities:
This method will work for any animal with a fairly straight back, whether it stands on four legs or two. Make a zebra, a cow, a kangaroo, a dog, or a bear.

Paper people can be made the same way. Look at the king on p. 55.

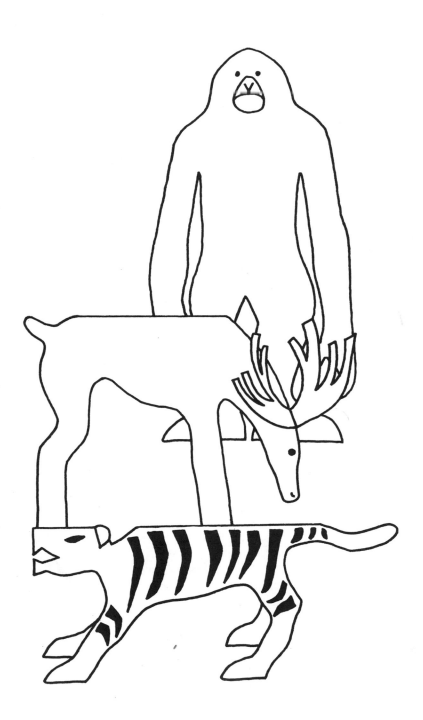

Interlocking Alligator

Materials Needed:
construction paper
two small pieces of oaktag or thin cardboard
green paint or a green felt-tipped marker

How to Make It:
1. Fold a sheet of green paper in half the long way. Cut out
the alligator's head, body, and tail, with the fold along the top.
Open up the head, but leave the rest of the body folded. Glue
the folded halves of the body together, or fasten them with tape
so that they won't open.
2. The unfolded head is just the upper jaw of the alligator.
Make the lower jaw by cutting a piece of construction paper in
the right shape and gluing it in place under the upper jaw.
3. Cut two sets of legs from the oaktag or cardboard. Paint or
color them green. Make a slit halfway down the middle of each
leg pattern.

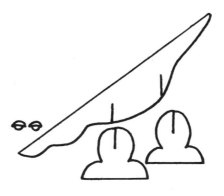

4. Decide where the legs should be attached to the body. Cut slits halfway through the body, from the bottom up. Slide the slits in the legs into the slits in the body so that the pieces interlock and the alligator can stand on its feet.

5. Make eyes out of colored paper and glue them onto the head. You can use beads for eyes to get a more lifelike look, and draw or paint a scaly pattern on the alligator's body.

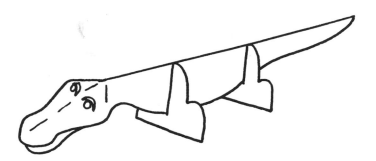

Other Possibilities:
Almost any animal can be made by this method. Look at the lions (p. 82) and the bareback rider's horse (p. 78). Try making a cow, a giraffe, or any other animal that you can think of. The interlocking technique is also good for animals with horns or big ears, which can be made of separate pieces that fit onto the head.

Tissue-Paper Birds

Materials Needed:
colored tissue paper
a small paper bag, or several paper towels
Magic Tape
pipe cleaners, coat hanger wire, or any
    fairly stiff wire
pliers (if you are using wire)
a black felt-tipped marker

How to Make It:

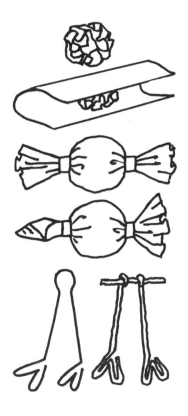

1. Crumple a few paper towels or a small paper bag into a tight ball. Place the ball in the middle of a sheet of tissue paper. Fold the tissue in half over the ball. Twist the ends, so that the ball is wrapped up like a party favor or a piece of candy. Fasten the twisted tissue with tape to make sure that the ball will stay tightly wrapped.

2. Fluff out one end of the tissue paper to make the bird's tail. Twist the other end tighter, bend it into the shape of the bird's neck, head, and beak, and hold it in place by wrapping it with tape. Draw two round black eyes with the marker.

3. The illustrations show two different ways to make the legs.

If you are using pipe cleaners, make two separate legs and attach them securely to a third pipe cleaner, wrapped around the base of the tail.

If you are using wire, you can make the legs all in one piece. Bend the wire with pliers to get the shape you want. You can use the pliers to cut the wire, too. Just bend it back and forth several times, quickly, and the wire will break. To attach wire legs, slip the base of the tail through the circle at the top of the legs and squeeze the wire with pliers.

Other Possibilities:

Make several birds, using different kinds of paper, with shorter or longer legs. Cut wings and tailfeathers out of tissue paper and make each bird look completely different from all the rest.

Bear-Cub Mask

Materials Needed:
a paper plate
medium-weight white drawing paper
string
Magic Tape
looseleaf notebook reinforcements
a crayon or chalk
felt-tipped markers

How to Make It:
1. Hold a paper plate in front of your face and use a crayon or chalk to mark the spots for eyeholes. Cut out a small round hole at each crayon mark. Hold the plate up again to make sure the holes are in the right places. Enlarge the holes a little at a time until you can see through them easily.
2. Set your compass for a $2\frac{1}{2}$ inch radius and draw three circles on white paper. Cut out the circles. Slit each circle from the edge to the center. Form the circles into flat, wide cones, and fasten them with tape or staples.
3. Tape on one cone to make the bear's nose. Tape or staple the other two cones to the back edge of the plate to make the ears.
4. Stick on looseleaf reinforcements just

below each ear, about ½ inch in from the edge of the plate. Punch holes with the compass point through the centers of the looseleaf reinforcements. Put a 1 foot length of string through each hole and tie large loose knots. If you pull the knots too tight, you might rip through the edge of the paper plate.

5. Color the mask with markers. Place the mask over your face and tie the strings in a bow at the back of your head.

Other Possibilities:

Use triangular ears and long paper whiskers to make a Halloween black cat mask.

Make a wolf or coyote mask by using a long, thin cone for the nose and adding pointed ears and white paper fangs.

Giant Giraffe

Materials Needed:
newspaper
a large roll of wide masking tape
paint, brushes, and acrylic medium

How to Make It:

1. Roll eight or ten sheets of newspaper into a tight tube. Fasten the middle and ends with tape. Wind tape around the entire tube, covering it completely.

2. Roll up two more tubes the same size and wrap them with tape.

3. Bend one tube to form the head, long neck, and body of the giraffe. Bend the other two tubes in half to make two sets of legs. Fasten the legs to the body. Start with a few strips of masking tape to keep the parts in place; then wind around enough tape to hold them securely.

4. Trim the legs, if necessary, to make them all the same length. Roll up small pieces of newspaper to make the antlers and tail. Crumple pieces of newspaper to make the bumps on the antlers and the thick brush of hair at the end of the tail. Wrap the finished antlers and tail with tape. Use more tape to attach them securely to the giraffe. Be sure the giraffe can stand without wobbling. Strengthen

parts that bend too much by wrapping
them with more tape. Wind tape tightly
around the bottoms of the legs to make
hooves.

5. Cover the giraffe with a coat of acrylic
medium. Paint the animal and then cover
it with a final coat of medium.

Other Possibilities:
Make a monkey with a long, curling tail,
a horse or a zebra, a snake, or a crocodile.

Butting Billy Goats

Materials Needed:
thin, stiff cardboard
tracing paper and carbon paper
paper fasteners
an ex-acto knife or single-edged razor blade

How to Make It:
1. Draw a goat's body and two legs directly on the cardboard. Trace the shapes you have drawn (see p. 13). Turn the tracing paper over, put carbon paper under it, and transfer the patterns to cardboard to make a second goat and another pair of legs.
2. Use the knife or razor blade to cut out the two goats and the four legs. Be careful cutting around the horns.
3. Cut two long strips of cardboard. Lay out the two strips and the goats the way they appear in the illustration. Make dots with a pencil to mark the three spots on each of the legs where holes are needed. Use a compass point or the tip of a sharp knife to make the holes in the legs. Now put the legs back in

place. By pushing the pencil point down through the holes in the legs, you can mark the correct spot for the holes in the strips and in the body of each goat. Make these holes, too, with a compass point or a knife.

4. Hold the parts together with paper fasteners. When you slide the two strips back and forth, the goats charge and retreat.

Other Possibilities:

Make a mother animal (any kind) with two or three babies walking behind her. When the cardboard strips slide from side to side, the animals appear to be walking.

A row of dancers, holding hands, sway back and forth when you move the strips.

Papier-Mâché Dragon

Materials Needed:
papier-mâché supplies (see p. 11)
toothpicks
masking tape
a sharp kitchen knife
one thick slab and one thin slab of styrofoam (available in
  hobby shops)

Preparations:
Tear two or three old newspapers into long strips, about 2 inches wide. Soak the strips overnight in a bucket of water. If your worktable doesn't have a waterproof surface, protect it with several layers of newspaper and waxed paper. Papier-mâché dries slowly, and painting takes time too, so it may be three or four days before your dragon is finished. A large, fat dragon might take as long as a week to dry.

How to Make It:
1. Cut the body of the dragon from the thick slab of stryrofoam. Your dragon doesn't have to look exactly like this one. Make the body longer if you want, or make a dragon that stands up on its hind legs, leaning back on its tail. Cut pieces from the thin slab of styrofoam to make the legs, head, and tail. Hold the pieces in place on the body by pushing toothpicks through them and wrapping them with masking tape.
2. Put about one cup of water in a bowl. Sprinkle in wheat paste, a little at a time, stirring with your largest paint brush. Keep stirring and adding paste until the mixture begins to thicken.

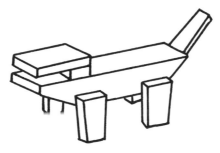

3. Brush paste onto the styrofoam framework. Lift out one strip of wet newspaper and hold it for a minute, so that the excess water drips back into the bucket. Wrap the strip around part of the framework. Brush paste over the strip. Wrap more strips around the framework until it is covered all over with several layers of paper and paste. Smooth the paper tightly against the styrofoam with your hands.

4. Build up the rounded shape of the dragon. Dip strips of wet newspaper into the paste and crumple them in your hands. Press these wads of paper into place on the framework, gradually building up the shapes you want. Wads of wet paper are heavy, and they tend to sag or drop off before the paste has time to dry. To prevent this, wrap each part of the dragon, as soon as it's finished, with a few more layers of long paper strips. Squeeze and smooth the dragon with your hands to get a firm, even surface. Wash out the brush with warm water and soap.

5. Wait one full day before adding the smaller details like eyes, fangs, claws, and horns. Make these parts by dipping small pieces of newspaper in paste and squeezing them into the shapes you need. Paste them onto the dragon and give the whole thing another coat of paste. Then set it aside to dry. It will dry more quickly if you put it near a radiator, or in direct sunlight. Use a cookie sheet or a large roasting pan to catch any water that drips from the papier-mâché.

73

6. Check the dragon as it dries, and glue down strips that start to curl up or come loose. When it's completely dry it will feel hard and very light. Cover it with a coat of acrylic medium. After the first coat dries, paint the dragon. Let one color dry before putting on another, unless you want to experiment with colors that run togther. With acrylic paints you can add as many layers of paint as you want, covering up mistakes and starting over again. Other kinds of paint may crack and flake off if they're applied too thickly, so use just two or three colors. For a glossy, tough finish, cover the dragon with a final coat of acrylic medium.

Other Possibilities:

Starting with a framework of styrofoam, you can make any animal of papier-mâché. Just arrange the pieces to get the basic shape of the animal, and cover them with paper and paste.

If you enjoyed working with papier-mâché and want to get ideas for more things to make, take out a book on the subject from the library.

PAPER CIRCUS
Circus Rings and Flags

Materials Needed:
oaktag or poster board
scraps of colored paper
felt-tipped markers
drinking straws

How to Make It:
1. Cut the oaktag or poster board into strips 1 inch wide. Glue a few strips together to make one long strip. Roll it up to see how big a ring it will make. You can make a small ring for each act in the circus, or you can make one ring big enough to hold the whole circus. Add more strips until the ring is the size you want.

2. Before gluing the two end pieces together, decorate both sides of the long strip with markers or colored paper cutouts.

3. Tape a straw to the ring to make a flagpole. Cut flags from scraps of paper and glue them to the flagpole.

Circus Clown

Materials Needed:
colored paper (any kind)

How to Make It:
1. Draw a circle with a 3 or 4 inch radius. Cut the circle out and cut it in half. Roll one half of the circle into a cone and fasten it with glue or tape.
2. Cut a collar from paper of a different color. It should be big enough to fit over the top quarter of the cone.
3. To make the clown's hair, cut two small rectangles of paper. Curl them the long way. Fold back a narrow strip at one end of each rectangle. From the opposite end, make a series of cuts, right up to the folded-back strip. Glue a fringe of hair to

each side of the head. Be sure the collar is on before you glue on the hair.

4. The nose, eyes, and mouth can be drawn with markers or made with flat circles of paper, tiny cones, and cylinders. Add buttons, bows, pockets, or whatever other details you want, cut from colored paper.

Other Possibilities:

Make several clowns using various kinds of paper. Give each one a different face and a different type of hair. Try making a collar by wrapping a strip around the neck, or give one clown a silly-looking hat with a feather in it.

Bareback Rider

Materials Needed:
stiff white poster board
tracing paper and carbon paper
an x-acto knife or single-edged razor blade
crayons or felt-tipped markers

How to Make It:
1. Trace the patterns on pages 79 and 80 and transfer them to poster board.
2. Protect the tabletop with a piece of wood, an old magazine, or a thick pad of newspapers. Cut out the patterns with an x-acto knife or a single-edged razor. Cut slits along the dark lines.
3. Color the horse and rider (and the horse's legs, too) with crayons or markers. Color both sides of each piece.
4. Fold the leg pieces in half. Fit the legs onto the body. Use a little transparent tape, if necessary, to hold the pieces in place.

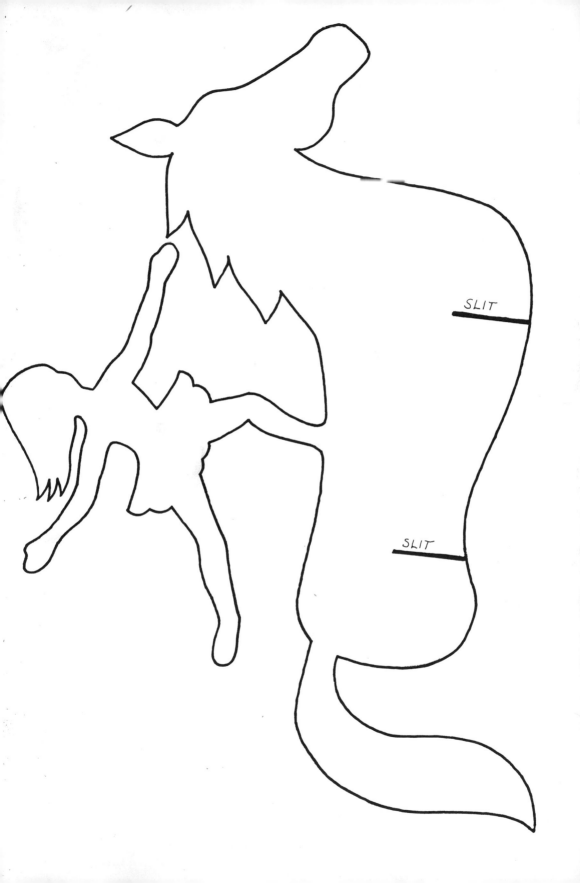

SLIT

SLIT

Other Possibilities:

Almost any animal can be made the same way as the bareback rider's horse. Look at the Interlocking Alligator on page 62 or the lions on page 82. Try a camel or a pair of zebras, or anything else you want to add to the circus.

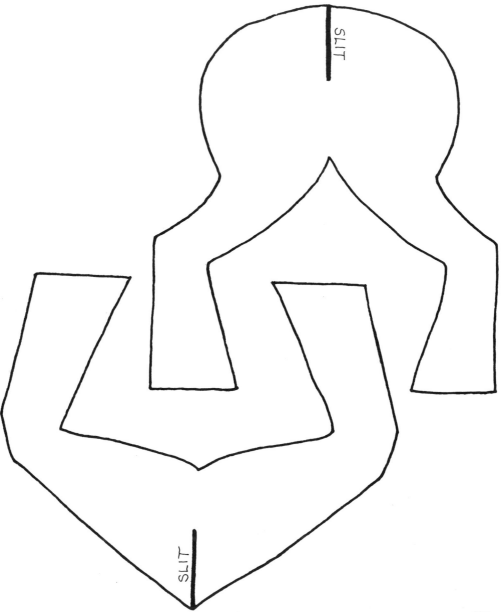

Elephant Parade

Materials Needed:

large sheets of construction paper or medium-weight drawing
  paper

How to Make It:

1. Draw the elephant pattern on a sheet of paper, as shown in
the diagram. Cut out the elephant.

2. Bend the two sides around and staple or tape the back legs
together. Curl the trunk slightly upward.

3. Cut two ears from scraps of the same paper you made the
elephant from. Fold back a tab along one side of each ear and
glue the ears to the sides of the head. Cut two long curved
tusks of white paper and glue them to the inside of the body,
sticking out a little on each side of the trunk. The eyes can be
little paper circles or dots made with paint or a felt-tipped
marker.

4. Make two or three more elephants, in different colors and
sizes, for your elephant parade.

Lions

Materials Needed:
thin cardboard or thick colored paper
felt-tipped markers or crayons

How to Make It:
1. Draw the four parts of the lion pattern on the cardboard.
There's no need to worry about how realistic your lion looks. If
it has a bushy mane, a long tail, and big paws, it will look fine.
2. Cut out the four parts. Cut the slits and fit the parts together.
3. If you want a sitting lion, just cut the slits in the body so
they slant forward instead of straight up. Make the rear leg piece
a little shorter and wider.
4. Color the lions with markers or crayons.

Other Possibilities:
Make a couple of folded paper tigers, like the one on p. 60, to
add to the circus.

Lion Tamer

Materials Needed:
construction paper
felt-tipped marker

How to Make It:
1. Cut a 6 by 4 inch rectangle of white or tan paper. Roll it up, the long way, into a cylinder. Fasten it with staples. Cut away part of the paper at one end of the cylinder to make the lion tamer's legs and feet. Before cutting, make sure that the stapled part will be in the back.

2. Cut a rectangle of bright-colored paper, big enough to wrap around the lion tamer's body and overlap slightly in front. Cut out a V-shaped section from the bottom of the rectangle to make two pointed coattails. Wrap the coat around the lion tamer and glue the two upper corners together in front. To keep the coat from sliding up and down, fasten it with a staple in back.

3. Cut the arms and hands from a strip of paper of the same color as the coat. Curl this piece slightly and glue it to the back of the coat.

4. The hat is a cylinder of colored paper sticking out of the top of the head. Fasten it in back with a staple or glue. Cut a

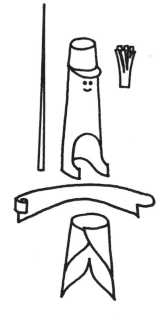

curved visor to fit the hat and attach it with paper tabs and glue. The plume is a paper fringe folded in half, and then in half again, and glued to the front of the hat.

5. Draw the face with a felt-tipped marker. Cut a colored paper button and glue it to the front of the coat. The whip is a long, tapered strip of black paper, curled slightly. Roll up one of the lion tamer's hands and glue the wide end of the whip inside the rolled-up hand.

Other Possibilities:

Make a circus band, with three or four figures in fancy uniforms playing paper instruments. A short cylinder, covered at both ends, makes a drum, and horns can be made from tiny tubes and cones of gold paper.

Ringmaster

Materials Needed:
black and white paper
Magic Tape

How to Make It:
1. Cut a 4 inch square of black paper. Roll the top two corners toward each other and glue them together. This will be the ringmaster's cape.
2. Cut a 4 inch square of white paper. Roll it into a cylinder just big enough to fit through the opening at the top of the cape. Push it partway through, so that 1 inch of white shows above the neckline of the cape. Fasten the white cylinder in place with glue or staples.
3. Use a compass point to gently poke a hole in each shoulder. Enlarge the holes with a pencil point until you can push the pencil in one shoulder and out the other.
4. Roll up a 5 or 6 inch long tight tube of black paper. Push the tube through the holes in the shoulders. Center it so that both arms are the same length. Wrap some Magic Tape around the ends of the arms, then bend them at the shoulders and elbows.
5. Cut a 6 inch square of black paper. Make the legs by rolling both sides in

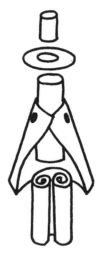

toward the center. Roll the legs tight enough so that you can stick them up inside the white cylinder. Push them in as far as they will go. Fasten them with a little bit of glue. Lay the figure on its side for a while so the glue won't run down the legs. When the glue is dry, stand the figure on its feet. If it doesn't balance just right, either trim the legs or glue them to a small square of black paper.

6. Cut a black doughnut-shaped hat brim that fits tightly around the top of the head. Attach it with two or three small paper tabs folded down inside the head and glued. The rest of the hat is just a black cylinder stuck down into the head and glued in place.

7. Glue on eyes and a mustache cut from black paper.

Other Possibilities:

Make a cowboy in a wide-brimmed hat, a striped shirt, and a vest, twirling a paper lariat.

Make an Indian maharaja to lead the elephant parade, wearing a long white robe and a colored tissue-paper turban wrapped around his head.

SCHOOL PROJECTS
Bulletin Boards

Decorating a bulletin board is a good class project. Everyone can help with the work. You can make holiday displays and signs about special events in school, or you can use the bulletin board to illustrate subjects you're studying. Here are a few ideas for bulletin boards.

Current Events Collage:
Use words and pictures cut from newspapers or magazines to illustrate the latest events in the news. For more variety, make your own paper letters, and add cut paper shapes, like airplanes, buildings, flags, or soldiers.

Science Display:
Make a model of the solar system, with a paper sun and planets on a black background. Stick on gold and silver stars to indicate galaxies floating in space.

Nature in Action:
Use a painted background or pieces of colored paper to show a cross-section of a hillside, or the shoreline of a lake or stream. Make paper cutouts of the plants and animals that live in the kind of area you're showing.

Costumes

Hats:

A well-made paper hat can really make a costume look authentic. Always use strong, thick paper, and fasten the parts securely together with tabs or tape on the inside of the hat. Use colored paper, or paint white paper.

A witch's hat is a simple black paper cone on a paper brim. Make the brim, try it to be sure it fits over your head, and roll up a cone that will fit the brim.

For a Pilgrim's hat, cut off the top of the cone and add a paper hatband.

Use a high cylinder instead of a cone for an old-fashioned tophat. Both this and the Pilgrim hat look fine with the top open, but if you want to you can cut a circle to fit the top and tape it in place from the inside.

A tiara is a jeweled headband worn by women on formal occasions in many parts of the world. To make one, just cut a strip of paper that fits across the top and sides of your head. Cover it with silver or gold paper and glue on decorative paper cut-outs or imitation jewels from the five-and-ten-cent store. Hold the tiara in place with bobby pins.

Bonnets go with many costumes, from clothing worn by New England Pilgrims

to that of western pioneers. The shape of the bonnet can vary, but it is easiest to use a semicircle of strong paper, big enough to fit over the top of the head and ears. Glue a scalloped strip along the front edge. Punch holes at the side and attach string or ribbon ties.

For an Indian headdress use a strip of paper that fits around your head. Fasten the ends together. Glue two paper feathers together with a straw or pipecleaner between them. Tape the feather to the head-band.

Other Possibilities:
Make a nurse's cap, a chef's hat, a fireman's hat, a knight's helmet, or a crown.

Clothing:
A mask or a distinctive hat is usually the focal point of a costume, but sometimes you can make the costume more realistic by adding paper clothing. You don't have to be exact in every detail. Often a collar or a sleeveless tunic creates the desired effect. Since paper is cheap, you can try different ideas without spending a lot of money.

Start with a long section of the plain white or brown wrapping paper that comes in big rolls. (It's sometimes called Kraft or butcher paper.) Make a hole big enough so that you can slip the paper over your head and fold it down in front

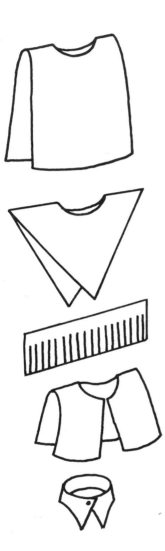

and back. This tunic is the basis of many different costumes.

Make a coat of mail for a knight by gluing on overlapping rows of large silver or gold paper circles. Be sure to start at the bottom. The same technique can be used to make the scales of a fish or reptile. To make the job of cutting the circles easier, just fold up the paper and cut several circles at once. If you're making an animal costume, glue on overlapping rows of curled paper strips to suggest fur, or paint the tunic to get the pattern you want.

For a military effect, make the tunic extra-long, held by a belt around your waist. Glue on paper buttons in front and fancy braid at the shoulders. A long brown belted tunic and paper fringes safety-pinned to your shirt sleeves will give a Wild West look. For an Indian costume, paint Indian designs on the front and back of the tunic.

To make a vest just cut a short tunic and slit it open in front. Cut it very short and open in front for a Pilgrim collar. Other collars can be made of wide paper strips cut to the right shape and wrapped around the neck.

Costume Jewelry:

A strip of strong paper is all you need to make a bracelet or a choker (a wide, tight

90

necklace). Cut a strip the right size and decorate it with colored paper, paint, felt-tipped markers, or cut-out designs. Put it around your neck or arm and fasten it with transparent tape.

To make papier-mâché beads you'll need newspaper, wheat paste, drinking straws, and fine sandpaper. Cut strips of newspaper 10 or 12 inches long, 1 inch wide at one end, and tapered to a point at the other end.

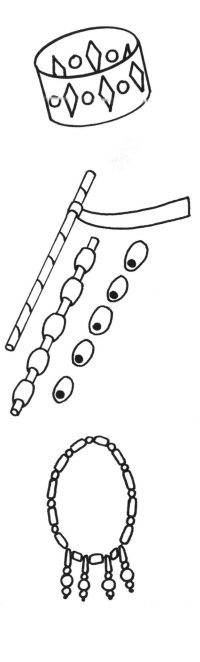

Hold a strip under water, then dip it in a mixture of paste and water. Starting at the pointed end, roll the strip of newspaper tightly around a straw. Pat the bead into a rounded shape. Use two or more strips of newspaper to make bigger beads. Leave enough space between beads so that you can smooth the edges with your fingers.

Set the beads aside to dry. Check them in a few hours and smear a little paste or glue on any that seem to be unrolling. It may take two or three days for the beads to dry completely. Sand them with fine sandpaper, then paint them whatever colors you like.

When the paint is dry, cut away the sections of straw between beads. String the beads on twine to make necklaces, belts, bracelets, headbands, or earrings. You can also sew them onto clothing in decorative patterns.

Other Ways of Life

Indian Village:

Use a piece of plywood, masonite, or thick cardboard as a base. Cut a mountain skyline of cardboard and fasten it, standing up, along one edge of the base.

The tepees are cones of white or light-colored paper. Cut off the tips of the tepees, and cut an oblong doorway in each one. Use drinking straws or straight, dry twigs for the lodgepoles. Paint the tepees with Indian designs and arrange the twigs or straws so they fan out at the top.

Make campfires of painted straws or half-burned twigs, with red and orange paper flames. The horses can be either flat cardboard cutouts or smaller versions of the interlocking horse on page 78. Cut a few flat cactus or tree silhouettes and make them stand by gluing down folded paper tabs.

Make the people of twisted pipecleaners. Paint them tan, and glue on paper hair, clothing, and feathers.

Other Possibilities:

Make an Eskimo settlement, with dog sleds, folded paper dogs, and papier-maché igloos.

Make an Arabian tent encampment, with paper camels resting in the shade of paper palm trees.

In a city of the future, show how you think people will be living fifty or a hundred years from now. Will there be helicopter traffic jams? Underwater bubble cities? Settlements on the moon?

Scenes from History

The Monitor *and the* Merrimack:

In 1862 the *Monitor,* a Union ship, met the Confederate ship *Merrimack* in the first battle between armored warships. Neither could do much harm to the other, but the fight marked a turning point in history.

Make the sides of the ships from strips of blue or gray oaktag. Cut oaktag decks, pointed at both ends, and glue them in place with tabs. The *Merrimack* had a large deck structure with portholes, a flat roof, and a smokestack on top. The *Monitor* had a revolving turret sticking up from the deck. Both ships had flags flying from flagpoles.

Build up the shape of each ship with oaktag, and roll up tubes of black construction paper to make the smokestack and cannon barrels. You might use some fluffy cotton to look like smoke coming out of the smokestack.

Paint a piece of cardboard a greenish-blue ocean color. Glue blue oaktag waves, standing up, along the edges of the cardboard.

Other Possibilities:

Make the first boatful of Pilgrims stepping ashore in Massachusetts, with their ship at anchor in the bay.

Another project is the winter camp of George Washington's army at Valley Forge, with rows of tents and soldiers hauling wood or huddling around the fire.

INDEX